This journal belongs to

_____

DATE

_____

THIRTY DAYS TO JOY

All Scripture quotations, unless otherwise indicated, are taken from the Holy Bible, English Standard Version, ESV® Text Edition® (2016), copyright © 2001 by Crossway Bibles, a publishing ministry of Good News Publishers. All rights reserved. Scripture quotations marked (NIV) are taken from the Holy Bible, New International Version®, NIV®. Copyright © 1973, 1978, 1984 by Biblica Inc.® Used by permission. All rights reserved worldwide. Scripture quotations marked (NKJV) are taken from the New King James Version®. Copyright © 1982 by Thomas Nelson Inc. Used by permission. All rights reserved.

Trade Paperback ISBN 978-0-7352-9082-2

Copyright © 2017 by WaterBrook

Cover design by Kristopher Orr; cover image and interior illustrations by Laura Elizabeth Marshall

Published in the United States by WaterBrook, an imprint of the Crown Publishing Group, a division of Penguin Random House LLC, New York.

WaterBrook® and its deer colophon are registered trademarks of Penguin Random House LLC.

Printed in China
2017—First Edition

10 9 8 7 6 5 4 3 2 1

SPECIAL SALES
Most WaterBrook books are available at special quantity discounts when purchased in bulk by corporations, organizations, and special-interest groups. Custom imprinting or excerpting can also be done to fit special needs. For information, please e-mail specialmarketscms@penguinrandomhouse.com or call 1-800-603-7051.

30 DAYS TO Joy

A ONE-MONTH CREATIVE JOURNAL

30 DAYS TO Joy

WATERBROOK

Discovering Joy

Joy and happiness are often treated as synonyms, but joy is so much more than simply feeling happy. Happiness is the feeling you get when the guy in front of you pays for your coffee at the drive-thru or your boss lets you off work a bit early. Joy is something you feel deep in your soul.

Although the pages that follow will help you discover what joy means to you, take this book as seriously or as lightly as you need. While there are a few questions that will specifically direct you to write, draw, or doodle, feel free to engage with this journal however you prefer—maybe you'd rather include a photograph or a collage. There are no wrong answers or methods here—all that matters is that you're choosing joy every day!

You'll notice two pages at the end of this journal to write down songs that speak to you every day during your journey. Once you've written out your full playlist, please share it. Create it on Spotify and tweet it to @WaterBrookPress using #JoyfulPlaylist.

Are you ready to begin?

Happiness and other feelings are fleeting, but joy has an origin and a Creator.

JAMILYN R. HULL

How is joy different from happiness?

I thank my God every time I remember you. In all my prayers for all of you, I always pray with joy.

PHILIPPIANS 1:3–4, NIV

Who are the people who bring you joy
and brighten your day?

A man has *joy*
by the *answer* of his *mouth,*
And a *word spoken*
in due season,
how *good it is!*

PROVERBS 15:23, NKJV

Use these two pages to depict joyful memories.

Weeping may tarry for the night, but joy comes with the morning.

PSALM 30:5

How can you remain joyful
in troubling situations?

Joy comes in sips, not gulps.

SHARON DRAPER

How would you depict something joyful
to others without using the word *joy*?

Joy is not the absence of suffering.

It is the presence of God.

ROBERT
SCHULLER

DAY

6

What settings or locations bring you joy?

Joy
is
strength.

MOTHER
TERESA

What is your favorite dessert?
Describe or draw it and write out
the list of ingredients.

Make a joyful
noise to the LORD,
all the earth;
break forth
into joyous song
and sing praises!

PSALM 98:4

What songs make you feel joyful?

Rejoice always,
pray without ceasing,
give *thanks*
in all circumstances.

1 THESSALONIANS 5:16–18

DAY
9

Sketch joy on these two pages.

Worry never robs tomorrow of its sorrow, it only saps today of its joy.

LEO BUSCAGLIA

In pencil, write those things that most frequently steal your joy. Next, in a colorful pen or marker, write ways you can choose joy in those situations.

There is not one little blade of grass, there is no color in this world that is not intended to make men rejoice.

JOHN CALVIN

What is your favorite color?
Fill these two pages with things that are that color.

Joy does not simply happen to us. We have to choose joy and keep choosing it every day.

HENRI J. M. NOUWEN

DAY

12

Choosing joy is easier said than done.
How can you choose joy every day?

There are souls
in this world
which have the gift of
finding *joy* everywhere
and of leaving it
behind them
when they go.

JEAN
PAUL

DAY

13

Portray your favorite weather
on these two pages.

Joy

is the

infallible

sign of the

presence

of *God.*

PIERRE
TEILHARD
DE CHARDIN

Look up from the page.
What's the first thing you see that brings you joy?
Draw or describe it.

Joy is the holy fire that keeps our purpose warm and our intelligence aglow.

HELEN KELLER

Fill these pages with doodles.

*Light shines
on the
righteous
and joy
on the
upright in heart.*

PSALM 97:11, NIV

Write down and illustrate a quote
or a Bible verse that brings you joy.

Joy, not grit,
is the hallmark of
holy obedience.
We need to be
light-hearted in what
we do to avoid taking
ourselves too seriously.

RICHARD J. FOSTER

Depict a silly memory from your childhood
in words or pictures on these two pages.

You get more *joy* out of giving *joy* to others, and should put a good deal of thought into the **happiness** that you are able to give.

ELEANOR ROOSEVELT

We often work hard to appear happy
even when we're struggling on the inside.
Think of ways you try to feign happiness.
When you see your friends and loved ones
doing the same, how can you reach out to show
them love and bring them joy?

*This is
the day that
the LORD has made;
let us rejoice and
be glad in it.*

PSALM 118:24

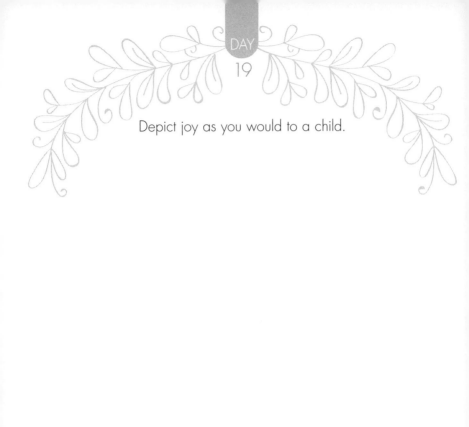

Depict joy as you would to a child.

You will show me
the path of life;
In Your presence
is fullness of joy;
At Your right hand
are pleasures
forevermore.

PSALM 16:11, NKJV

DAY

20

What is a truth that always brings you joy?

Man cannot live without joy.

THOMAS AQUINAS

Fill these two pages with words or images
that make you smile or laugh.

The LORD is my strength and my shield; my heart trusts in him and he helps me. My heart leaps for joy, and with my song I praise him.

PSALM 28:7, NIV

Illustrate a song lyric that makes you feel joyful.

Embrace *relational* uncertainty.

It's called *romance*.

Embrace *spiritual* uncertainty.

It's called *mystery*.

Embrace *occupational* uncertainty.

It's called *destiny*.

Embrace *emotional* uncertainty.

It's called *joy*.

MARK BATTERSON
*In a Pit with a Lion
on a Snowy Day*

DAY

23

Using words or images,
create a joyful picture of your future.

The greater part of our happiness or misery depends on our dispositions, and not upon our circumstances. We carry the seeds of one or the other about with us, in our minds, wherever we go.

MARTHA
WASHINGTON

In what ways do you find that your disposition affects your spirit when you're experiencing tough times?

Joy is the simplest form of gratitude.

KARL BARTH

Fill these two pages with gratitude.

Comparison is the thief of joy.

THEODORE ROOSEVELT

In pencil, write out traits others have that you wish
you had. Next, in a colorful pen or marker,
cover them with a list of your qualities
that make you who you are.

There is *no joy*
in the *soul*
that has forgotten
what *God*
prizes.

OSWALD
CHAMBERS

Reflect on a time in the past when you felt truly joyful.

Do not be
grieved, for the
joy of the LORD
is your strength.

NEHEMIAH 8:10

If joy were a person in your life,
who would it be and why?

The LORD has done great things for us, and we are filled with joy.

PSALM 126:3, NIV

Fill these pages with things that make you feel joyful.

Joy to the world, the LORD is come! Let earth receive her King.

ISAAC WATTS

As you've spent the past month reflecting on joy,
how has your outlook on life transformed?
How has your view of God
or your relationship with Him changed?

But the fruit
of the Spirit is love,
joy, peace, patience,
kindness, goodness,
faithfulness,
gentleness,
self-control;
against such things
there is no law.

GALATIANS 5:22–23

Create Your Playlist

Create your own joyful playlist here. You can either come to these pages each day to jot down a song that is speaking joy into your life that day or write down all at once your ideal playlist for adding joy to your life. Music has a unique way of activating our memory, so put together a playlist that will encourage you to choose joy each day and to remember the journey you took while writing in this journal. Once you've filled this out, we'd love to hear the playlist you came up with. Create your playlist on Spotify and share it with us by tweeting it to @WaterBrookPress using the hashtag #JoyfulPlaylist.

1 Song: _____   6 Song: _____
   Artist: _____   Artist: _____

2 Song: _____   7 Song: _____
   Artist: _____   Artist: _____

3 Song: _____   8 Song: _____
   Artist: _____   Artist: _____

4 Song: _____   9 Song: _____
   Artist: _____   Artist: _____

5 Song: _____   10 Song: _____
   Artist: _____   Artist: _____

11 Song: _____

Artist: _____

12 Song: _____

Artist: _____

13 Song: _____

Artist: _____

14 Song: _____

Artist: _____

15 Song: _____

Artist: _____

16 Song: _____

Artist: _____

17 Song: _____

Artist: _____

18 Song: _____

Artist: _____

19 Song: _____

Artist: _____

20 Song: _____

Artist: _____

21 Song: _____

Artist: _____

22 Song: _____

Artist: _____

23 Song: _____

Artist: _____

24 Song: _____

Artist: _____

25 Song: _____

Artist: _____

26 Song: _____

Artist: _____

27 Song: _____

Artist: _____

28 Song: _____

Artist: _____

29 Song: _____

Artist: _____

30 Song: _____

Artist: _____

What I have learned about myself:

Where do I go from here?

About the Author

(Write your autobiography here.
Include your photograph, if you'd like.)

Acknowledgments

I would like to thank the following people
who have helped me discover joy:

Acknowledgments

The development team would like to thank all the individuals and departments within the Crown Division and WaterBrook for their help in creating this project, in particular Pam Fogle, Karen Sherry, and Julia Wallace.

Development Team

Kendall Davis

Jessica Lamb

Kristopher Orr

Sara Selkirk

Susan Tjaden

About the Illustrator

Laura Elizabeth Marshall is the owner of the Etsy shop DoodlingForDays, where she sells a variety of inspirational prints and designs. She has a heart for missions, and 100 percent of her Etsy proceeds go toward local and international mission work. Her talents include painting, design, and illustration, as well as custom chalkboard and calligraphy art. Laura is a first grade teacher and lives in Houston, Texas.

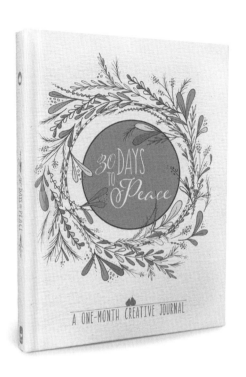

THROUGH BIBLE VERSES, QUOTES, AND ARTISTIC PROMPTS, THIS CREATIVE JOURNAL INVITES YOU TO THE DEEP PEACE GOD OFFERS YOU EVERY DAY.

See sample pages and more at WaterBrookMultnomah.com

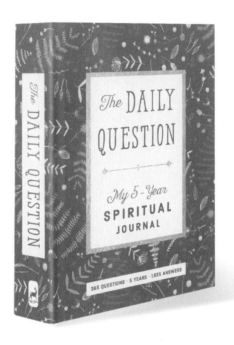

A THOUGHT-PROVOKING, 365-QUESTION GUIDED JOURNAL
THAT SPARKS DAILY REFLECTION ON FAITH AND
LIFE OVER A FIVE-YEAR PERIOD.

See sample pages and more at WaterBrookMultnomah.com

WATERBROOK